Hazel Smith | Word Migrants

New Poems

GIRAMONDO POETS

Hazel Smith | Word Migrants

First published 2016
from the Writing & Society Research Centre
at Western Sydney University
by the Giramondo Publishing Company
PO Box 752 Artarmon NSW 1570 Australia
www.giramondopublishing.com

© Hazel Smith 2016

Designed by Harry Williamson
Typeset by Andrew Davies
in 10/16.5 pt Baskerville

Printed and bound by Ligare
Distributed in Australia by NewSouth Books

National Library of Australia
Cataloguing-in-Publication data:

9781925336030
A821.3

All rights reserved.
No part of this publication may be
reproduced, stored in a retrieval system
or transmitted in any form or by any means
electronic, mechanical, photocopying or
otherwise without the prior permission of
the publisher.

In memory of my mother Eta Cohen
and for my sister Maureen Smith, violinists both,
and for my husband Roger Dean, also a musician

Poetry books by Hazel Smith

Abstractly Represented
Keys Round Her Tongue
The Erotics of Geography

Contents

The Forgiveness Website
3   The Disappeared
5   Experimentalism
8   Soundtracks
11 Train Talk
12 The Great Egret
14 Slowly Time is Moving Fences

The Poetics of Discomfort
19 Verdict
21 The Poetics of Discomfort
24 Blow-up
26 Feasting on Belshazzar
29 Disagreement
30 Tennis Court Ode
31 SnowTalk
32 Asylum
33 Feisty and Childless (an internet cut and paste)
35 The Bleeding Obvious (an internet cut and paste)

Mismatch
- 41 The Wrong Tom Jenks
- 42 The Cud
- 43 Underbelly
- 45 Mix-ups
- 48 Tennis Elbow
- 50 Choice
- 53 The Zeds and the Dees
- 55 Student-Teacher Relations
- 57 The Educator
- 59 Encounter
- 60 Afterimage
- 61 Addressed
- 62 Whatever Love Means
- 64 Negotiating

The Shivers from Analogy
- 69 Metaphorics (in three parts)
  - 1 Metaphor (an internet cut and paste)
- 71 2 The Unanswered Question
- 72 3 Windfall (A Polylogue)
- 75 The Blue Bus
- 78 The Chairs

80	The Club
82	The Other Room
84	Revolutions
85	Screen Saver
86	Art for Whose Sake?
87	Flow
89	Subvoices
91	What You're Doing, If You Know (after Robert Wilson)
92	Feelings and Algorithms
94	Clinch
96	Tilt

Erasures

101	Disappearing
103	Aftermaths
105	Ubasuteyama
107	The Women of Calama
110	Siteless
113	The Decision
118	Notes
126	Acknowledgements

The Forgiveness Website

The Disappeared

Before you disappeared sometimes I barely noticed you. You were solid, but the rhythm of your breath wasn't always a point of focus.

I rarely thought of taking photographs or writing down what you said. Why replicate the given?

Before you were taken away I was always full of joy, but there was often something strong-smelling and distasteful in the distance. I never knew whether you could smell it too.

Words pulled up to stations. I avoided noisy crowds. Most of my thoughts were hardly worthy of appropriation.

Before you were blown apart we sometimes disagreed. It was our way of consolidating.

I read about the disappearances in the newspaper: the lynchings, the dawn raids, the men in vans. It could be media-speak but I wished I had the courage to rise up. I relied too much on the heroism of others. Perhaps secretly I was reconciled to liquidation.

Before you disappeared my aloneness was the vibrations of a coastline, I could feel the pitches of the waves beneath my feet. Now the soles of my feet sink into the sand. And it sticks.

I knew we weren't immune. I consulted every website and manual. I gave you instructions knowing you would throw them away. Not to play certain notes, not to sonify your dissidence.

Once you dissolved, the disappeared kept gathering. They came from all over the world. They stacked up in the doorway and the driveway, and hummed fragments of your compositions.

It put an end to grieving. For the first time I understood the low tones you bequeathed me.

Sustained beyond reverberation, resonant beyond deafness.

Experimentalism

one of Dr Mengele's ex-twins
decided to forgive him

experiments carried out
beyond the limits of the medical

two tiny girls
leaving the camp in 1945
at the front of the line
it's famous footage

years later after Miriam died
Eva met with another ex-Nazi
even found she liked him
they walked arm in arm at Auschwitz

a body lies beneath her
its organs plundered, measured
she wants to disconnect it

but can she write blank cheques?
'you can't cash in the suffering of others'

(for Eva unloading the past was trial and error)

there is a forgiveness website
where you can download
though they never tell why you should
or how you to do it

– forgiveness: it reeks of the theological
there must be a better word –

some say it's reciprocal
but faced with the real-time
grievances of Palestinians
Eva's negotiating skills quickly withered

there was a lot of banging on the table

recently I decided I would blame myself
for everything that happens to me
suddenly the world seems
manageable, lighter, freer

and delay becomes a vanishing act
as we apologise for stealing other people's children
some saw their mothers again, others didn't

when I came home from school each day
I always needed to embrace my mother
immediately, that moment, without waiting

even Miriam and Eva
(at the front of the line, holding hands)
could cleave to each other

Soundtracks

Music is about memory, but enduring is about forgetting.

They'd cut off your hair but you could summon up the tresses, tap them into a poem.

At first the boots felt like a threat, a reminder of surveillance. They came too close, the wall a spineless membrane. But then you started to need, even desire, them. Punctuation of the night, grammar of dismantled senses.

The feet become a face. A house burns into light. A careless guess becomes a premonition.

What country are we hovering over, you say, as we hurl into outer space. Is this a heatwave or a blizzard? A microphone sways in the wind trying to find an ideal position. Geography becomes an art form, rising from its own ruins.

The walls of the rooms are severely dented with urgent, unidentified knocking. A plane continues to soar and swoop but can't find the courage to land. It could be a warning or a confession, it could be desert or savannah. You hear a chord faintly in the distance: a destination or a rejigging?

You kept asking where we were going and demanding to see a map. It was below zero, the wind swirled then dispersed, the horizon oozed unease. We took the first road, and even though it didn't seem to belong to us, we kept on going.

Unquenched, we walked past a field of discarded keyboards. The river was switched off though flowing. In the distance the ocean, fatally wounded, groaned. Time swayed like an out-of-orbit drunkard. The earth was studded with torn dollar bills, broken lamps and carcasses.

They blindfolded us at the borders, confiscating our propositions. But they could be kind too: first patrolling, then caressing. You look quite different from what I imagined he said, but what was he expecting? My anger flared then cooled. Faces needed to be reassigned, eyeballs removed from their sockets.

But there were so many partitions! Whichever one you were behind, the action seemed always to be on the other side. You opened a door, walked in and left words swaddled and abandoned on the doorstep. Those were the days when you still believed you could unhinge the future and rezone the past. But you weren't supposed to, and the punishments were always the same, though disguised in fashionable colours.

They gave me the soundtrack of my life, no images, just noise. Listen to it, they said, then report back on what you find, there are no metaphysical limits. I can't listen without looking, I said, and I can't interpret without seeing. They weren't the right words, I turned my back. Someone took out a gun and fired.

Sometimes I dream I have murdered someone, when I wake up I'm not sure if I have or haven't. It's the boots again, though smaller than before, laced-up, polished. Often I hear them walking on their own, limping but locked in. They persist but they aren't deafening anymore, more like an old man shuffling.

Train Talk

the lost man cannot be retrieved
to lose is not to be at a loss
the man had suffered a slipping away of his
own, his homeland

    you don't normally talk to men on trains
    the man confounds, his strange allure
    steps off, the wheels of the train dissolve
    absence presses the open button

        it was the silent carriage
        you weren't supposed to be talking.
        you shared the unfolding, the dumb haze
        of exile, a windless knowing

            to recover from loss requires a loosening
            of the loop, lop-sided, labile tracks
            loom as the longed-for station

    the search spills over with
    headless questions crack open
    subterranean thirsts blow through
    the tousled hair of reasoning

loss recharges then loses speed
traces don't surface by drawing lots
to mourn the missing is not to be mindlessly driven

The Great Egret

      the black car patrols the banks

      the border slices through the river
          overflows with the
      blood of the slaughtered

         the families in hiding
         hatch out of the trees
      in which they are nesting

         unveil the young bride
         in white wedding dress

         on the opposite bank
         the black-suited groom
      his face blurred by distance
         flies his flag high

  a minister mimes the gapped rites
      the couple walk in a circle
      but not round each other

         the bride throws her
         veil into the river
         the groom hurls
         his flag into the flux

the veil, the flag
swim to each other

their miscegenation
ejects a great egret

stands on one leg
stabbing for prey

flock of white feathers and yellow billed
its neck poses questions

the great egret is not a stork
but it is a witness
its eggs a nation's regrets

the patrol car explodes
wedding march gunfire
the guests flee, disperse

the egret flies off into the blue
across rivers, across deserts, across grassland

Slowly Time Is Moving Fences

Fences are relocating themselves, and the moon comes to rest on my computer laptop. You cling to a suggestion you know you will eventually evict. I can't write like that anymore she said. Bake another kind of cake, richer and smoother.

I'm being awkward again, but there are so many ifs and buts. Is that sound laughter and if so what does it mask? Old age coughs terminally, darker than chaos. When you fear something, do as much of it as possible, he said.

Beneath the renovated surfaces someone is dropping coins into a bucket. In a weak moment she allowed the family secret to escape. I continue to surf – the sea, the internet, other people's thoughts, anything that will keep me buoyant. Meanwhile, sexual fantasies seem to keep the economy afloat.

Somewhere in the next town they are putting babies up for adoption. The crowds gather, as if for a mass-rally or an execution. Every year they switch apartments, cats and software. They hold a warming party, anxious about the mathematics.

The reality show has been faking it all day. He knew she was discussing him with her therapist, and it annoyed him because everything she said was untrue and he couldn't fight back. You should write about what interests you was my advice to her but she said she didn't know what that was. She never answers, ever, that's the basis of our correspondence.

Once you have given up everything, you can reconsider small matters like the direction of your life. You tell yourself not to say the wrong thing and then you do. It's perverse, inept, could it be deliberate? But that's music for you, so much more than sensory delight. Back in the eighteenth century, the castrato's high notes tremble.

The Poetics of Discomfort

Verdict

the barristers of reality don their wigs obliquely
each conviction the child of previous acquittal

'it was a different social climate then'
'at the time they weren't legally guilty'

'what they did was wrong then and is still wrong now'
'no atonement beyond self-pity'

she flinches from this
harassment of the past
but she also backs off from
pragmatic smothering

> she had never been abused
> or had she?

>> she runs the rusty algorithm
>> pours the dried-up potion for the assay

there was the man who touched her up in the queue, the man who stood outside her room waiting for her, the man who took her outside and threatened to kiss her, the man who put his hand down the back of her blouse, the man who pushed himself against her on the tube, the man who was teaching her to drive and put his hand on her knee.

there was the piano tuner who demeaned her, the decorator who bullied her, the colleague who insulted her, the flashers on the underground and on the other side of the street

        the parameters were still adjusting
        wayward beyond statistical averaging

        sniffer dogs on the scent
        of messed up sixties liberalism

she had not been abused

Or had she?

The Poetics of Discomfort

the microfictions of your life
are walking awkwardly

she balances on crutches
slowly shifts her weight

feet trail their east
and west protuberances

props herself against a post
and shakes her phone out

you wonder if you should
you hesitate and wonder

everyone is ignoring her
and you know what it's like
to be ignored

do you need assistance?
No, followed by a full grimace

a mistake made knowingly is more
a booing crowd demands refunds

you are angry with yourself and
irritated with her for being irascible

returning home
a disability activist on TV
admonishes the very kind
of heinous act you've
just been perpetrating

along with others
or their more felicitous inversions –

the deaf speaker
lip-reading your question
from the deep north of the lecture theatre
then lithely returning it

or years ago in class
you didn't know
whether to ask the girl
with cerebral palsy to perform
her poem out loud

an ordeal for her and for the class
agog at your insouciance
their mute cheers spurring on
this literary paralympian

pleased or displeased to have
read the poem out

slow to respond
when you ask her
can I publish it?

Blow-up

the right to intervene doesn't understand its own agendas
or the birth defects of its 1989 delivery
could war ever be eliminated, the girl in glasses asks
a soldier guns down a deserting algorithm

they met again
in the room before the gas chambers
he could intercede, tell her
where she was heading

it would mean certain death for both
better to embrace her
let her sleepwalk into execution

'a device to be manipulated'
human rights drew first breath
in the look-up files of anti-communism

'why don't you ask him to change his plans
if it's so depressing for you'

'that would be interfering, Georgina
and I don't interfere'

well I do, but there can be consequences.

he had been interfered with as a child
endured parental meddling

sharing, my ain folk, a place you can call your own

editors, teachers, tweeters, bloggers
we are all interventionists now

shoot me but not my writing she cried

I'm not committed, he said
to what poetry can incite
only to saving defenceless words
from detonation

somewhere someone is scribbling
a book about genocide
that is a genealogy of waking

Feasting on Belshazzar

For Emma

'Mene, Mene, Tekel, Upharsin'

I tend to mix my biblical stories up
thought it was Nebuchadnezzar not Belshazzer
who saw the writing on the wall

The Euphrates dried up but
the Red Sea parted at the seams
is that it?

the camp sprawls below the stage
heads bob out beneath the curtain
the chorus shifts from Jews to
Babylonians to Persians

these days they would all be dieting not feasting
or selling off the plundered temple vessels

I wondered how the writing
magically alighted on the wall
hand of the director, not divinity

Cyrus repatriated the Jews
And, some say, respected the customs and religions
Of the lands he conquered

invented the first declaration of human rights
(others claim the Cyrus cylinder was merely
Mesopotamian propaganda)

the kings like today's politicians
began their reigns with
ambitious and unlikely-to-be-implemented
declarations of reforms

If only statecraft was similar to stagecraft
an exercise in eyeless threading

God threatened to take his scissors to the kingdom
half to the Medes, half to the Persians
biblical cut and paste
or first two-state solution?

enter the twentieth century
the so-called Great Powers
(latest line in meddling foreign dynasties)
hacked up the Middle East in ways that
ripped belonging

Saddam started building over Babylon
extinguishing the gasping scraps
of antiquarian living

to be continued

the faltering prophesies
the tapestries of killing

'thou has been weighed
on the scales and found wanting'

in the endgame are our incisions

Disagreement

disagreement is the driver for seeing other points of view
each day you reverse your intentions into cloudy, no-through codes
a conversation with the dead becomes resuscitation of the missing
as the rotting of the word became flesh, email bred facebook
    begat twitter
the chimpanzee organised stockpiles to shore-up evolutionary stoning
she defended typographical chaos with mellifluous dyslexic singing
how to respond if multinational corporations start to finance
    the aleatoric
the stench was outsourced to operators who morphed it into noise
the pitch flux of the cosmopolitan, the sound-surround of belonging
highways through the hitched together, the return of the
    spurned repressed
a volcano vomiting like a child avenging parental absence
she allowed herself an annoyance fix to inject a sharper calm
the race toward entropy surges before its target shrivels
as the missing card stutters to life in an already downsized pack
the moral high ground shakes off soil, slays addiction to the written

Tennis Court Ode

you can join in any conversation without really knowing the score
the garlic on the ghost's breath was deposited on the letters
push back the boats they cry from the decks of miscarrying vessels
a foetus sticks its head out and then retires to fallopian bliss
that which is salient I have found is usually that which is hidden
as dementia starts to cut its teeth, secrets begin to throw racquets
a technician unplugs the autocue as an aid to the autoerotic
he made others feel he was dependent on them even though
    he wasn't
off-shore processing, onshore protests, people-smuggling poetics
writing becomes like death row with stochastic bouts of remission
sometimes he said I find myself not liking people who everyone
    seems to admire
the doctor talks and talks though he's taken an oath to listen
as a stranger swivels on his bar stool and knocks over the carefully
    poured drinks
the jury decides it wants to go home and serves a hit-and-run missive
it's the time of hanging on parliaments and hung-up prohibitions
it's the time of backstabbing and net-rushing, of re-combinative
    commitment
the anxiety of influence, the passivity anxiety breeds
she took the headscarf on and off unsure about metaphor's limits
as the poem becomes as breathless as an asthmatic culture permits
a voice from a convex mirror shouts, 'he's the John Ashbery of tennis'.

SnowTalk

the seasons are talking to each other
we pick orchids in the snow
as if the world's thermostat
was programmed for cross-weathering

fairylights frame the Hindu temple
shops sell gift-wrapped buddhas
they gorge themselves on Christmas day
then purge at Ramadan

did you know that snowflakes are irregular?
that words shiver when they boil?
as the white wind fills its tiny lungs
it hears black trumpets blowing

shall we rewrite the brothers Grimm
so Snow White is mottle-skinned?
the reindeer is exhausted
the sun burns up the sludge

Asylum

...whatever these people are fleeing, whatever circumstance makes them think they'd be better off chancing death on boats hardly worthy of that description, we must offer them something worse. That something is Papua New Guinea.
Waleed Aly, 21 February 2014, *Sydney Morning Herald*

whatever feeling they are fleeing
makes them think death hardly
worthy of description drives

an off-chance fleet of boats
can make them dream
of choice, of fleeing

circumstance however wordy
claims off-shore the certain
death-bed of their freedom

desperate people circumscribe
description think that
they'd be better off on boats
not knowing that the worst is
what we offer

Feisty and Childless (an internet cut and paste)

A long time ago I decided that I wasn't going to have any children. People need to feel they're right, and have to convince everyone else that they are. We suppress other biological urges: nobody thinks fidelity is 'weird'. E-researchers have found that people derive more satisfaction from eating, exercising, shopping, napping, or watching television, than taking care of their kids. Looking after the kids appears to be only slightly more pleasant than doing the housework.

A long time ago I decided that I wasn't going to have any children. We're used to childless women running things, they used to be called nuns. Did you 'just know' you wanted to be a mother? Well I 'just know' I don't. I do worry about being lonely when I'm older. I pursue volunteer work for charity, I give blood, I've offered to donate my eggs. Look, I like kids – I just couldn't eat one whole.

Childless women subvert discourses round constructions of femininity. *As a mother myself*, meaning that only women with children have real feelings. A filmmaker, talking to the *New York Times*, probably is more comfortable discussing her films than her uterus. First Romeo wants to marry Julia. I have experienced first-hand the effects of bad parenting, and I don't want to perpetuate that.

My partner doesn't want kids. I lack the appropriate resources. I was never drawn to dolls. I wonder why I am so ambivalent about my own status: why at times I feel myself a lesser being, even as I despise anybody who sees me that way.

'I think having children is the greatest experience of any lifetime.' My childhood was enriched by a childfree uncle, who took us to galleries and films we would not otherwise have seen. There is a constant drip, drip, drip of pressure, a need to justify your self in a way parents never have to do. If childbirth and rearing are so bloody essential, why do so many abortions happen every year? I am on constant alert, fearful of the stray remark or image that will rock my equilibrium.

A long time ago I decided that I wasn't going to have children, and a long time ago the world decided I wasn't, because I didn't have children. The time has just gone and it was or wasn't a long time ago for time is short. And in short, I am not sure whether I decided to have children or not, maybe I did and maybe I didn't.

The Bleeding Obvious (an internet cut and paste)

In an age in which no topic appears prohibited, menstruation remains utterly beyond the pale.

Women are likely to bleed for between 2,250 to 3,000-plus days across their lifetimes.

In 2013, 'menstrual activists' are tasting, baking and making art with their own menstrual blood as a gesture of defiance.

Tampons are not particularly well-regulated in terms of their pesticide and dioxin content that will fill both landfills and oceans.

The world's first official menstrual-themed poetry slam is dubbed 'Red Howl Moon'.

In the African-American hoodoo tradition, as well as in Sicilian folk-magic, menstrual blood served to a man in his coffee or tea is a sovereign recipe for capturing his sexual attention.

Menstruation is a matter for private lives, not public exhibition, so few museums collect artefacts associated with this defining occurrence in women's lives.

The most glaring example of period blindness occurred during the Boston Marathon in 1996, when the winning female athlete Uta Pippig ran with visible menstrual blood and severe cramp.

Activists are questioning the medicalisation of premenstrual syndrome and the over-prescription of anti-depressants to treat its symptoms.

All polygons are two-dimensional figures and when we talk about menstruation in Math, we use measurements to find the area of fields in different shapes with different dimensions.

Alluding to menstruation in music is about as ground-breaking as playing in a sandbox.

In Sumba, women keep their cycles secret, which makes men see them as deceitful.

Free bleeding is when a woman decides not to use feminine products in exchange for allowing her blood to flow 'freely' out of her body, staining her clothing and running down her thighs to wherever it may end up.

Several plane crashes in the 1930s had involved menstruating female pilots, and experts – male experts, of course – suggested that putting a woman with 'menstrual disturbances' in the cockpit was an invitation to disaster.

Given the low-gravity environment of space, some scientists wondered about the possibility of 'retrograde menstruation'.

Returning women astronauts who've menstruated in space report that everything worked the way it usually does.

Mismatch

The Wrong Tom Jenks

I looked him up on the internet but it's the wrong Tom Jenks
histories banged together, homepages for high jinks
the past repeats as it permutes, but also rejigs the past
welcome to the mix and match of discombobulated planes
to cross is not only to traverse, but also to conjoin
organisms tear apart the niches they construct
earthworms are proto-alchemists, they switch the soil to gold
a jumble, a mosaic, a mix-up, a montage
conversations build a cartography that maps an alien field of art
nations bounce back from combat into an adaptive ache
agendas pulse erratically, expectation swings its chronic beat
she amputates accusations, screws on prosthetic myths
he felt attracted by her one day and repulsed by her the next
variants are deviations that play bad tricks on genes
revamping your story is unwise but it doesn't mean certain guilt
a treatise resolves as tea-leaves, fragments disarm her fists

The Cud

as the day is passing out, night slowly starts to chew the cud
her mind migrates promiscuously, staggering into out-of-place
rhythm brings buoyant chaos to the bovine morning's themes
clarity loses suppleness, asynchronous, ungainly, stiff
last night there was a violent ticking that couldn't be ignored
timelines came and went by overland express
the planets seem stateless as they hold the stars apart
surrealism is old-fashioned but has an up-to-the-minute look
the books you never wrote are published to stuttering acclaim
everything is pure conjecture but contamination rules OK
the piano finds new octaves that are off the keyboard map
he pulls on geographies at random until the rule of reach implodes
in a crime scene overrun with voicemail that is locked
poets download verdicts, declare generic guilt
the bones of a young woman float at sea for curious fish to poke
the nagging purr of morphing whales, the porpoise of extinction

Underbelly

as insistent as an algorithm
it pursues a strident pulse
has no arms but holds you in position tightly

shakes you up
but doesn't shrug its shoulders
rarely listens though its ears twitch
exhales stale breath as if it were a fragrance

Made from syllables but not words. A not-language, a non-land.

The first time she performed it, she was overtaken by what she had raised up, the accent she had adopted. Her eyes started to dilate; the distance between the sounds and her collapsed.

The moment had found a migrant inside her and was pushing it out. And a stranger outside was coming to meet her.
Finnish, Lithuanian, Welsh
but also the cut and pasting of passports.

She performed the language often, she inhabited it as home
but it never had the same effect on her again.

the child only a child myself 1960 clinging to her mother she'll be better off with parents who can look after her the couple much older they had to be a Jewish couple only a child myself don't remember what they looked like didn't realise the child only a child myself they talked her in a single mother without money she'll be better off my aunt looking for her name in the wedding lists it's a terrible thing to take a child away from her mother my mother wails the child only a child myself clinging to her mother's dress realised didn't realise crying

Minutes after the train crash, he shed his clothes, wallets and mobile phone. He walked away, shutting down thought or expectation.

Hours after the train crash, the wish to reassign, the promise of the not-yet-mapped.

Days after, a recycled ghost, he returns with buttered lies.
The life he has abandoned, his new adoptive home.

Mix-ups

Culturally, no 'Asia' exists, and the peoples who inhabit 'Asia' often have little in common with each other.
A sign in the Asian Art Museum, San Francisco

Philosophically, there is no definitive blue; the sky is always salted with clouds.
Chronically, we sort words into piles, stitch up the scattered mess of the senses.

Sometimes she speaks fluently, sometimes she stutters. She feels connected to her visitors, but doesn't know how they relate to her or to each other. She forgets a great deal, but she remembers what absorbs her.

She keeps saying she is sad because she hasn't had any babies.

They retort, again and again, we are your babies. She says, I think I'll adopt one, and they laugh and throw it back, how could you adopt one when you need people to look after *you*?

She thinks she lives upstairs. She is sure there is an attic. Shuffled, beyond the control of buttons. She is forced to improvise; the habitual is crooked.

She weeps and weeps saying her father has just died. He is in the next room and she has neglected him.
They claim she will never learn anything new again. But she does, and last week did better in her memory test.

out of the soup of ideas you pick the most aromatic pare them down until you reach the core grows smaller disappears have to call it back by pulling on its fragrance

out of the soup of illusions you pick out the mongrel looks most like you lower her voice grainy rough resistant

into the soup of impossibilities you stir inter-stellar stardust

as the soup is about to be served you snap the ladle

If you have never killed someone you won't know what this is about.

That day the elevator wasn't working so I took the stairs. There seemed to be thousands of us like refugees, there was barely room to climb or breathe. I was anxious in case the stairs collapsed under our collective weight. Outside the sky was blue but the streets were homogenous grey. I knew I had murdered someone, and that murder was something from which you didn't escape. The details should have been sharp, but instead they were pale and vague.

It had happened, but everything suggested it hadn't.

As I was walking a woman appeared and begged me to take the child she was holding. The child's skin and eyes seemed to suggest she wasn't Caucasian. I wanted to take the child, it was as if she was mine; the woman's pleas were loud and urgent. But I couldn't because I knew I had killed. If you have killed you can't look after a child, everyone knows that. I turned my back and walked faster and faster, until I could no longer hear her pleas. When I turned round the woman and child had disappeared, though I seemed to still see them.

Sharp and vague, this sense of loss, this sense of connection.

Tennis Elbow

rain stopped play
yet there seemed to be momentum

a boy divorced his father
then adopted several strangers

a woman woke to find her
English accent Asian

the net was up and down

there were other setbacks
that turned out to be advances

someone said she didn't want to have a child
there was no applause
the relief was palpable

someone else complained about the smell of semen

there were TV programs
no one ever mentioned
trophies champions disowned

it was all a mismatch

war broke out

his backhand burst in fragments

Choice

It was the night before the reading and as usual she couldn't decide what she should perform. Once you put your hand in the jar, it was quickly lost amongst the bits.

Poem A was permanently ailing, Poem B couldn't stay in one place. D and E were in-your-head poems and read out loud were sonically pale. She liked poem M but it seemed to rise from a past consciousness, like washing machines with a mangle or black-and-white televisions.

She had started writing something for the big night several times but it was all just starts. One day these starts might paint their own finishing lines, or pal up as a composite, but not by tomorrow night.

Poem S hinted at incest, T spoke of war. But most of them were not about anything at all. They were written in poem-speak, heads bobbing up and down, half-floating, half-sinking in a vast, glutinous, semi-buoyant mix.

Even if she stilled the poems, they had to be placed in line. Every poem would only hold hands with privileged others; they were promiscuous but within discriminating limits. Reversing the order was like living your life backwards. A dizzying experience but not exactly a blueprint for success.

Another poet (male) had suggested that she should put all the poems in a box, stir them round, then pull out a poem and read it. But she needed to sculpt her delivery, which this person who made the helpful suggestion certainly had not. He swayed from foot to foot, dropped bookmarks on the floor and mumbled incontinent intros, while he threw the dice about what to read next.

Should she pick her best poems or those that would best please? Or to put it more crudely, should her listeners come first or should their wishes be tuned out? She sensed her own beat, whereas every audience tapped into its own codeless asynchrony. Romancing their mobile phones, running up bills at the bar, they clapped, even cheered, but rarely seemed to be listening.

So to what would they tune in? Poem J was incomprehensible. Yet there were people who adored incomprehensible poems, you yourself were a self-confessed addict of this genre. But should non-addicts be made to suffer until they atoned their resistance?

If the dilemma came down to one point (and most dilemmas do), it was this. A poet was not an entertainer. And risk-taking didn't necessarily entice. But there was one of you, a really annoying one, but an itchy get-up-and-go-I-won't-be-put-down-and-behave-myself miscreant, that wanted your performance to connect.

Some thought the remedy was to make the audience feel as uncomfortable as possible. One of me would like to nurture *your* discomfort, but I'll try not to bring my selves into this.

Yet I would prefer your disdain to your affirmation. If you boo me it will steady my self-doubt. There are precedents for this, just as there is a history waiting-to-be-written about the poems poets evicted when they groomed others for promotion.

The poetics of the crookback, the lyric in the lean-to,
legs and arms poking out at gawky, buck-teethed angles,
the seasons stewed and stirred up, the ocean noisily emoting

between the cherry and the checkpoint, the conceptual and the corny,
the waiver in the wavering, the aesthetic as the awkward,
the flying trapeze of song talk, the big dipper of vocalese,
poetry as stalker somersaults as willing victim

        po-er-po-re-per   e-voco   cho-der   oive   ding
        vo-co-de ci-vo-co-ry   co-cho   ire   re
        in-vo-co-re   ear-tree   re-yrt-oc choi
        is-on-try   vo   cho-re-cis-on

        de-ci-di-ce-de   poing poing
        re-de-po-e-pa   choi cho
        e-po   och-re   oice

The Zeds and the Dees

Once a Z zoomed into view it was impossible to relax. Grit in your eye. Sleeping to an alarm. Dilly-dally and the Z would overtake you, crashing into the garage.

Zs were big bullies so the worst strategy was to surrender to them. But surrender you always did.

Usually there was not one Z but several. A Z gorged on list-making, bossed you onto buses. Priorities and subsets; accelerations and stop offs.

Not just lists but mathematics. How many days between you and the Z? How much to be crammed into a day, an hour, a minute? The unknowns: the infection that might slow you down, the unplanned catastrophe or visit. A cacophony of new Zs, pushing calculation into chaos.

On rare occasions a Z disappeared, only to reappear on the missing person's list.

It often woke you early in the morning. It waved its arms and kept insisting, 'If you get up now you can get ahead. So get up.' Rising early could spell later exhaustion, slowing time with sleeping. But a Z could also make you peddle faster.

Sometimes you wondered what hell would descend if you didn't meet the Z. Pilloried? Alienated? Excommunicated? Spat at? There were those that didn't meet their Zs with curiously few consequences, but that was other people. Sometimes a Z slid by silently without penalty or implosion. This didn't soothe your disquiet about the next one.

Some people thought a Z was only a Z. You didn't panic until the night before. Then you cut through the time that remained, mincing hours into minutes. But that meant no flotation: half-surfacing, half-sinking at will.

Sometimes the Z was a pleasurable perfume, a more potent version of vanilla or jasmine. This side of Zs always vapourised, but posed an unanswered question: whether you craved them as much as you hated them, whether Zs were an addiction.

Sometimes you set your own. That didn't always work. A Z was usually hammered down, the bolts screwed firmly into position. If you could open it out, it was something else: tractable, user-friendly. A real Z was self-centred, obnoxiously demanding.

Once a Z was sent packing, it always sent a pushy replacement. The next one was already stalking you, campaigning for your extradition.

Then there was the ultimate D that wasn't a Z because you didn't know when it was descending. That D you couldn't really prepare for, a Z without any payoff, the end of Zs as we know them. These Zs were only practice events, the palest of rehearsals.

Student-Teacher Relations

An American student, shrill and sure, upbraided me about my teaching, 'you should ask them to keep a journal, you know', exactly what I didn't want to do lest it lead them into the temptations of confessionalism, but I tried to look as if I had learnt my lesson, while also trying to firmly transmit that I hadn't.

Did you know that two per cent of prisoners make false confessions, and that they do it sometimes just to get a drink or a fag or to return home earlier, one chap even said he had done the murder when he hadn't so as not to be executed, an offbeat logic difficult for me to follow.

Though it depends what death is, how much one might try to avoid it. I think of it as locked-in syndrome, which is horrible.

Each day my teaching further lowered its voice, until I was just one amongst many holding back my comments, the students gave theirs sometimes honestly, sometimes dishonestly, because they didn't want to inject realism into camaraderie, or because they didn't want to encourage negative critique of their own poems.

'I'd like to be a violinist but I don't know if I'll ever be good enough.' Until she realised all she could do was keep on grinding. So she ground and ground until one day she was good enough, at which point the game was dust and she decided to embark on another bildungsroman as a poet.

I have some suggestions to make, he said, after the performance, implying that he as elder statesman hadn't liked it, and calling up the only power that audience members have which is to imply that they could do better.

I'm always amazed (aren't you?) by what folks are prepared to reveal or not: some pathologically private people will take their trousers down on TV, while everyone thinks poetic suicides are symptomatic, but you can't distil the poet from the poem, any more than you can understand what death is by scrutinising a corpse.

The Educator

For A

the days are broody
she cocks up her morning ear and stirs
it is time to do her email
and through a mist of typos to address the world
this morning she feels a little bruised
it is something someone said
what was it? an index of
the real or a map of
misadventure, a
footprint of the misaligned

she lacks sleep and is a little grey-faced
but knows that as the day hurries along
she will heal

then it's off to work
and as usual
the educator makes pedagogic haste
this morning she has been teaching
that whiteness is a form of
deafness (can be molded into listening)
until the door is firmly closed
and a pile of marking sweeps her up
in a mess of fails and high distinctions

at midday she
rhythmically chews her lunch
to the seminar speaker's wayward tune
more students and another class
the day draws in
it's time to write
she pulls books at random off the shelves
and from a witch's brew of
cut-ups, misfits, annexations
conjures up a wicked quilt

until it's yoga-time then home
where she flops from a day of dizzy busyness
leans back looks out to sea
and broods if only for a moment
on the high-pitched absence
swirls about the pulsing lack
the boom of the unauthored
tides stretch out their arms
then turn around

Encounter

Every conversation is a gentle misfiring
    An abacus points beyond method or counting
        An exchange derails, eyes averted, glancing

Every meeting invents its own detours
    A palette of sounds claims the outskirts of reading
        A botched translation, muddied inscriptions

Encounter recasts solipsistic thinking
    Words cool down while their brothers are bubbling
        Clay tokens change hands, war defines fiefdoms

Afterimage

Picture this: a young man on a bus and a young woman to whom he is talking.

Men are plentiful but scarce.

They barter thoughts, hover at the check-in of a feeling.

When the wheels freeze he asks her if she would like to go to his room for coffee.

She doesn't accept.

He is studying geography. She isn't interested in geography. She doesn't drink coffee.

Often she wonders why she didn't say yes. She is glad she didn't.

The flagged-down traveller, flaming.

Why recharge the waste-bin, why remix the ridden?

Addressed

n   a i s   g s r
h m bs m s c f n qu r
s   di ri b s
n p   i u s a d n i id a
g s h s t a i t w i r s a t

   win v srs a tii n wit h ast r ang s r
   wha m bsr m asi w ifs n qui r y
   shs d isri b ss
   ni pril igu s and n iwid a
   gas h sst a ikt i iiw i rds at tir s hsr

      cinv ersa tiin witn astr ange r
      cnam berm asic ifen quir y
      sned isrib es
      ni pril igue andn icida
      gash esta lkti iiwi rdsat tire ner

         conversation with a stranger
         chamber music of enquiry
         she disrobes
         no prologue and no coda
         gushes talk till words attire her

Whatever Love Means

Alex is in love with Bridget, but B is unsure whether she is in love with A. Alex declares his love but Bridget is not unzipped for such declarations. Alex is patient but is also determined to teach B a lesson. We can never really know what Alex is thinking, nor does he know himself. He starts to date Bridget's cousin Cath. Bridget realises (too late) she is in love with A.

Bridget adopts the role of martyr. She won't tell Alex about her feelings, because she doesn't think she should. She hides her inclinations but she leaks them slowly too. Somewhere sex kicks in: a babe in the womb, locked up.

Time passes, huge vats of it. Alex remembers the alphabet and complains to Bridget about Cath. Cath sports dowdy dressing gowns, is self-obsessed and had an affair with someone else. Alex isn't given to complaining, so this hands B the permission she's formerly lacked.

Bridget knows that Cath isn't really in love with Alex, just as Alex isn't committed to Cath. But someone has to tell Cath. She may feel betrayed. She has been used, no eliminating that. But betrayal can serve useful purposes, be the endgame everyone wants.

Alex hooks up with Bridget and they stick. Cath is on the canvas but is gradually painted out. One day, centuries later, Alex thinks he spies Cath on a train. She disembarks several carriages away: maybe it was somebody else.

The story of A, B and C grows smaller and smaller, until it is microscopic. It's a matter of opinion whether it entirely disappears. Bridget and Cath meet on a plane and decide to travel the world à deux. Cath is married to someone epic, much more suited to her than A. A slight edge always between B and C: the past happily burbling away.

Negotiating

she wants to go for a walk he wants to go to a film she wants to go away for the weekend he wants to stay at home she wants to buy expensive chairs he wants to buy cheapies each minute hour day whether you decide to do what the other desires sometimes stick out often give in enjoy surrendering *she wants him to make bread he wants her to make soup she likes the house warm he likes the house cold* need to visit his thoughts doesn't want visitors open windows keep them shut became what you want to do if you know what it is often didn't whether should put that first sometimes never always like to give in without resistance *he likes white wine she likes red wine she craves lentils he craves meat* tiny nugget of not wanting grows flares up dies down sorry a freedom in not doing what you want quickly turns into what you wished always as long as you did some of the time people make space way of thinking opens up new slant surprises *she prunes his thoughts he paints her feelings she feels washed out he washes up* fits with what you need to do what you don't sometimes fast forward the bits of the news she wants to watch mustn't ever assume someone is like you no point in interviewing that woman her brother has just died wearing makeup showing a lot more body bags body bags body bags *he likes to swim she swims to like she loves TV he hogs the ipad* no ceasefire the negotiator resigned if you don't like someone you don't shoot them need to know how people deal with misery might have to endure consider yourself lucky making trivial decisions he will give in the next day will not give in the day after that knowing someone so well you could almost predict what they will do next knowing you can never entirely know them never you entirely or themselves

The Shivers from Analogy

Metaphorics (in three parts)

1. Metaphor (an internet cut and paste)

Metaphors are comparisons between two dissimilar things. We think metaphorically, whether we're aware of it or not. Where would I find a sea filled not with water but with grief? The 'war against' metaphor creates an 'us and them' frame. *The ubiquity of metaphor in language has been established in a number of corpus studies, and the role it plays in human reasoning has been confirmed in psychological experiments.* Use *Metaphor* on your desktop computer or tablet device. His metaphor is performative – it enacts the undoing of his own gender. By the end of the course you will have learnt the role of metaphor in understanding the unconscious mind. He used a metaphor that made us cringe: licking the other side of the stamp. I want to argue against metaphor – against substituting one thing for another, to enrich or complicate our understanding. 'Why is it we say what something is by calling it something else?'

Use all metaphors, dead or alive, sparingly, otherwise you will make trouble for yourself. 'Those who foolishly sought power by riding the back of the tiger ended up inside.' During the treatment of violent individuals the authors noticed that physical assaults were often preceded by an onslaught of metaphors. There is no way to metaphorise the actual experience of losing any or all of your senses.

The metaphors for talking about sex in the US all come from baseball, let's talk about pizza instead. Music as metaphor: a powerful tool in leadership development. *It hurt the way your tongue hurts after you accidentally staple it to the wall. She grew on him like she was a colony of E. coli and he was room-temperature British beef.* You are welcome to your opinion of course. But these are metaphors and in the end are likely to be misleading.

2. The Unanswered Question

answers rarely fit with their questions

it was years since she'd wept, it was inexplicable

it's an odd sentence that doesn't commune with its own
    strangeness

the moon outsmarts every poem about it

I'm fired up he had said as the house burnt down brightly

her ideal script was never the one she composed

she googles her CV, it no longer fits

it was years since he had died, the crime scene was yellowing

facts lock in to the fictions we hang them by

3. Windfall (A Polylogue)

I don't know whether I want to shake my life into bits or grip it like a handrail. The lightest wind can cause the ball to swerve. It's a crossing of bumps and abrasions, missed stations and barred gates. Every day I slip on the dropped peelings of somebody else's intent.

The grail they desire was never conceived, not will the quest gestate. The black box is slowly liquidating, the ocean sucks in its own depths. I watched the news and didn't absorb the details, I surf by floating on my back. They suggested I write down my objectives, as if I knew what they were. If I knew, I wouldn't need to write them down I said.

There's no such thing as a goal, just whims; heresy defines the route. I'm an experimental poet she said, hoping cartographically that might fit. The moon outsmarts every poem about it, a compass pins words west and east. He's standing behind her, mapping what she writes, while a rhythm nods its unhinged head.

In poetry metaphor is everything; she wondered if she believed what she proposed. The rain saws the hapless day in half, the bark will keep the soil moist. Is it so new to them they won't understand or have they heard it all before? No self-help book ever worked it out. Her colleagues will never tell her what they really think. And the world wears indifference as its tell-all badge.

Ants in the sink in the morning, possums pounding on the roof. *Being helpless is his strategy.* The personal is like a violent toothache, while an earthquake on TV sidles by. You've never experienced genocide, she said, taking an unanswerable stance. Nobody noticed I was irate. There is a part of me that expects other people to read my feelings, while the other me knows they can't.

Death is a frame and you like the frame but not the object of embrace. You hang the clock in cock-eyed positions: you leave go whichever way it tilts. She said forgive me, but I didn't know what to say, because I hardly remembered the incident and there wasn't anything to forgive. She could be difficult in a thousand ways, but they never coincided with her own regrets.

He's not sure why he loses his temper, when he's always vowing that he won't. Breathe deeply, create a pause, then think how you really want to act. Authenticity is the game plan, but the rules seem suddenly inchoate. She confessed but I wasn't convinced. They kept saying I was buying too much food, but then when I didn't we nearly starved. The battered beat their own; but in art, repetition is sweet.

Sometimes I think the speaker is hopeless as he exits to rapturous applause. There is always thunder in the basin, a flare-up in midst of the field. Bask in the silence and celebrate, don't set fire to what you believe. Disdain will do the job as well as praise.

The Blue Bus

there are days when no one knows where the blue bus is
but there are always times when you know
it will arrive out of the blue
then you are riding amongst colours only, gone with the winding
saluting the destinations as they pass you by
making passing your destiny
the blue bus doesn't give you the blues
but the blues was banished by segregated bussing
the blue bus is neither bone nor skin, neither fever nor shivers
you remember other buses, the bus to school, the fears of being late
daydreams scribbled like automatic writing on muggy windows
the moment they lock the doors I want to jump off
it seems (though no statistical data can nail it) that more people claim
blue as their favourite colour than any other
whilst The Big Blue Bus is a municipal bus operator
in the Westside region of Los Angeles
today I decide to pretend that everything is what it is and is no other
it's odd the way we relish titles even though like people
they are divorced from what they hope they are conveying
you remember all the buses that came and went
the ones you nearly missed, or deliberately let slip
but most of all the buses that though appointed never appeared
it says on the blue website that blue symbolism
runs the gamut of emotionally-packed meanings
some of us have to write at speed to turn our recalcitrant wheels
the blue bus is what you imagine it to be

what you paint it to be, what you desire it to be
or so they say and as we know the saying is not the said
especially where performance is in the playground
sometimes the blue bus is just itself, pure blue
open to the seductions of sound
ploughing through the traffic jam of reason
sometimes it falters and becomes bus-like
reigned in by timetables and bus-stops, borders and controls
Rosa Parks stood up for sitting down anywhere on a bus
and for the rights of all African Americans
but there are those who say she appealed easily to whites
and could be smoothly assimilated by them
without any shifting of position
to write is to move, to think is to mutate
it's even a film, *Three Colours: Blue*, Kieślowsi, about a musician
the blue bus is sometimes made of clay
sometimes made of silk, sometimes made of feathers
but it always erects itself like a genie
from a transmutable yet sustainable bottle
it is run by an invisible collective who have hidden histories
of bizarre steering techniques, unorthodox
gear changes and tyre-kicking
usually when I ask where I can catch it
I am greeted by incomprehension bordering on suspicion
but it is the blue bus that takes me everywhere
even to locations I will never reach
and even into this excuse for
an improvisation which is not improvised

but draws on an improvisatory aesthetic
the blue bus, the horse and carriage of sparring avant-gardes
whipping with abandon through the galloping streets of black Britain
it's a funny thing, you know, but I can't remember
what the colour of the buses in Australia is.

The Chairs

You are upstairs reclining on the sofa.

It is late afternoon. There is a knock on the door.

Ten women are standing on chairs and are all performing identical movements. They carry frangipani branches and they rock the branches in their arms.

One of them steps off her chair and beckons to you. One of them even offers you a frangipani branch. The blossoms are very fragrant but you decline.

It would not be a good idea to invite them in.

The women disappear but they come back the night after. They sing and rock, rock and sing. You want them to go away though you also want to join them.

They return the next night and the night after.

Sometimes one steps forward and talks eloquently of the joys of gardening.

You wonder what you are missing but you are not really interested.

It's becoming tiring. Have they not noticed that you have no garden? But they are also kind and you do not want to turn them away.

They come night after night, month after month. They bring you cuttings.

You neither encourage them nor turn them away. They keep coming but less often. There are more silences between the chairs, and the frangipani blossoms seem a little less fresh.

Sometimes you just stay upstairs and let them be, downstairs, standing in a row, holding their beloved branches.

The Club

the woman who didn't have
what other people have
was looked upon
with fear with pity and with envy

they wanted her to long for
everything in which they had invested
craved an expression of regret
she couldn't give it

in every sphere there are the haves and the have-nots
the woman didn't speak of her have-knotted-ness
and they didn't ask her which surprised her

it's like a club
most people have joined up and
want to be reassured
they haven't wasted their money

how to explain what cannot be explained
it was not her decision only
it was not a decision at all
there were mumbled words she couldn't catch
strident voices framed in spotlights

there was so much more
closed in but banging on the sides
the intricacy of coupling
the companionship of art

how she disliked rules
ownership, possession
(to have must not be to hold on to)

but soon she would be
amnesiac, bedridden, alone
the hardest part was coming after her

The Other Room

I have two keys she said
that match Murakami's two moons

four hands move over the piano keys
the players deftly swapping
places on the makeshift bench

the poet and the critic trade
tee-shirts in the other

room unlocked
flung windows wayward spill

the dark of crying soothes
the ears of the paedophile

sever the baby from its twin

each moon colliding with
the other leaving one

an unpaired earring
hangs a problem on the crime
the code the scene

the keys could all be
replicas the kidnapped gives me

chills, the world of genres
is the world of fools

Revolutions

the well-crafted poems you despised are suddenly lacerating tradition
      a poet reports a breakthrough in postponing winter weather
a gorilla and a human mirror movements for each other

meanwhile the nation turns its eyes to lip-reading not literacy
         as the cube revolves, she's standing on the ceiling
  an angry listener invades the stage, snaps the performer's fiddle
wordplay dips its sonic pen in the blood of severed grammars

Screen Saver

They take you to a room, the floor is strewn with books. Some of the books seem duplicates, but are different books open at the same page. Other books have identical names, but variant pages.

Someone turns the lock, you are cut off.

In the middle of the room is a double-sided screen. You walk round it. Sometimes the two sides project a twin word, sometimes the words contrast. You wish that the screen would revolve or that you could gracefully pass through it.

The screen is too bright but there is no switch to turn it off. Everywhere, there are piles of books crammed round it.

If you hold up a page to the screen it scans it. But the words that emerge on the screen are not the words on the page.

You read about a pear and 'severed arm' appears. You think of a pear and 'pear' bursts open, quickly flips into 'knife'.

One night, men in hoods shoot from the screen. The books are rent with bullet holes; all you can do you is push your fingers through.

Hours pass, you rip out pages, fling them at the screen.

The words dislodge, spill like blood upon the floor.

Art for Whose Sake?

Mishka Henner, 36, a British photographer who collates in his gallery Google Street view images of places that prostitutes frequent has been nominated for a £30,000 art prize.

he is not interested in narrative but seriality

GIRLTALK uses the latest technology to bring to you the most sensual girls in town. Using your own computer you can have real time interaction with the girl of your choice. Ask for anything you want and she will supply it (without ambiguity)

what the project can show, he says, is quantity

when I pay for sex I don't expect to be considered responsible for the girls. I don't ask them anything about themselves. I don't think about what they are doing when I am not there. I don't expect to clear up their problems or repay their debts.

Tragedy and trauma the safe comfort zone

Henner googled internet forums to find out where prostitutes solicit and then captured their locations using Google's street cameras.

I loved it because it didn't pretend it was trying to understand the experience of the women.

An alternative form of documentary

The women are no longer there
The landscape has changed

parachute voyeurism soaked in a language of pity

He doesn't need to release the shutter

He does not share the traditional aesthetic of photography

glitch and blur

Detachment is perfect for his subject

Flow

It isn't flowing you said.
But nothing ever flows. It dribbles, wanders off, diverts.

    An empty room. A cough. Then the empty room again.

In the negotiations that led to that agreement, we had 700 days of failure and one day of success (George Mitchell on Northern Ireland).

Curiously pallid. Cold. Dehumanised.

    You said this isn't going to be my new direction
    but how would you know?
    you may be blown off course

    One of those buzz words. Used gingerly by academics.

Frog in the throat
    taking shape in slow mo
        low clouds overhang
hands-on diplomacy

    How about: there is never one solution but several?

    Untouched clay. Terra nullius.

(Perhaps activism always feels like this
curiously impassive, un-dynamic)

everywhere fanatics are spewing out fictions
    their crazy fingers glide across keyboards
    their thoughts as clear as H20

    the verbal show-offs are having a great day

'no conflict without resolution'

    a chair, a scarf, a door half-open

when I am drowning in desiccation
    when the commission fee is about to be returned
the missing piece shuffles awkwardly into position

Flow is OK, but sometimes we need to walk on ice.

Subvoices
for Robert Sheppard

'There's so much inscape in your poetry.' The chandeliers were out of breath. We were all trying to avoid any whiff of the pastoral. The subwoofer was burning socks.

Spit looped in pesky bullets, the police raided lyric lines. Those were the days when shock tactics outpaced their plastic hooks.

Once the chase was over, our insteps arched their backs. It's not funky anymore to be oblique. Smoking behind the mainstream, pancakes don't give a toss.

'You sound like Hopkins on speed,' he said, *and I don't think he meant drugs.*

Can you retrieve the system, now the chance procedures are lost? Those hammer-hugging deliveries, the readers lunging back and forth. The carpets were utopian but the audience rarely laughed.

As remix edges out collage, the local draws cosmic straws. The shepherd plays with his iPhone to mind his flock remotely.

Robots can't ever be Roberts, the conceptual can never seduce. But poetry can always be revived with in-vogue spelling salts.

On your advice I mashed words and music, shredding both to make them synch up.

The sonic out-wraps the saying, the canon is in it for kicks.

What You're Doing, If You Know
after Robert Wilson

Ify ouk now hati tis, w hatst hepo into fdo ing it?

I fyoukn owwh yy ouredoi ngsom ethingd ntdoit?

Ifyudk nowwh atyo uaredo i ngw hatist hep ointofd oningit?

Si vous savez ce que c'est, à quoi ça sert de le faire?
Hvis du vet hva det er, hva er poenget med å gjøre det?
如果知道是什么，还有什么好做的呢？

If you know what you're doing there is no reason doing it.
If you know what it is, what's the point of doing it?
If you don't know why you're doing something
or how to think about it

                                                          Do it

Feelings and Algorithms

a feeling and an algorithm
once upon a time
then suddenly a stranger embraces her

a feeling feeds an algorithm
once upon a tyrant
the strange forensics of story felling

resurrect an affect that was kneeling
in time once or twice upon
an empire, an emblem, an embolism

touchy-feely theft, a calculated shootout
once upon a bout of open wailing
wakefulness, lunacy, derangement

spattered but statistical
the poem as a crime scene
the mathematics of exuberant living

the hot kisses of equations as
testament, the half-connected dots of
known, unknown, cross-dressed, an algorithm

joy flaming envy programs rage morphs as relief
puns wrung from numbers, once upon a changeling
a system, the shivers from analogy, that strange embrace

unfettered, stepping out of self-imposed policing
once upon the digits that dial death
poetry in all its wily grace, feelings as algorithms

Clinch

when I broke my leg I placed
the pain in a distant corner
of the room and willed it
smaller and smaller

he embraced his grandmother
'no one hugs me anymore
one of the deprivations of growing older'

she didn't add 'you are more susceptible to tears'
or 'touched' can mean insane

in Thailand to pat someone's head is rude
in India, historically, the untouchables

knowingness of fingers over Braille
cool seductive surfaces of clay

media reports of diasporic
punching, kicking, strangulation

touched up, the figure in the portrait passed out of recognition
touché he said when she sketched in the impossible

words, the touchstones of literary unfolding
touchscreens, the death-row of writing as we know it

voices orbiting on their own, voicetracks pulverising each other
the bungled touchdown on the moon, the perfect swimming
    touch-finish

he brushed her arm and it meant everything and nothing
those twisting histories of embrace and prohibition

when the hairdresser massages your scalp it isn't simply cerebral
cuddling a child, he argued, is not the same as paedophilia

Tilt

Have they tried to straighten the leaning tower? Unlikely!

Tourist gold at stake; poetry at an angle.

The house is up a dangerous road. They negotiate the perilous bends with three-point turns, swerving from side to side. She's not a risk taker, and death responds eloquently to postponement.

A magnificent view from the hill-house, Tuscany's as good as they say. *Don't lean over the balcony, you could fall.* The bells are chiming melodiously off-key. Bells to the right, bells to the left ring asynchronously together.

There's always a point at which the poem could veer either north or south. You can't choose, because the road map hums on silent. Follow both till you reach the citadel: strident, luminescent.

She leans on him too much. He's dependable so it is easy to do. If she can't figure out the plotline, she knows he'll throw the dice for her, decide.

They hear a woman shrieking and shouting in Italian from the house next door. She doesn't seem to care that she is being overheard. How deep does her anger run?

Or is she only venting her feelings as we all must, through the ups and downs of the everyday?

Joan Retallack's poetics of the swerve, 'Unsettling transfiguration of once-familiar terrain'.

A straight bow, parallel to the fingerboard. It's the means to find a good sound: it's the way that you were trained. Violinists can play well with the angle skewed, but physics is not to be denied.

The words inside her risk falling over, without landing safely on the other side.

Below is a location map and aerial view of the Leaning Tower of Pisa. Using the buttons on the left (or the wheel on your mouse), you can zoom in for a closer look, or zoom out to get your bearings. To move around, click and drag the map with your mouse.

He couldn't climb the tower because he suffered from vertigo. Would the lean make that less or more?

When she held her back straight it felt strained. It seemed natural to bend forward, as if trying to find her way in life.

This was her problem: that she could always see events from another angle, one that didn't suit her point of view. But to be political you had to be mono-eyed.

His neck cranes slightly towards the left. It was the result of childhood surgery. Now it is part of what he is, the promise of a balanced life.

I'm inclining to one verdict rather than the other. But you can build a case either way. These retrospective prosecutions: they don't allow for the fact that people change.

It was begun in 1173 and the sloping was apparent before it was even finished. The engineer tried to compensate by making the new stories a little taller on one side. However, the extra weight caused the tower to sink even more.

The closer you come the less it seems to tilt. The moment you move away, the leaning is retrieved.

Backwards and forwards, equilibrium finds its sway.

Erasures

Disappearing

He needs to step out of his life and visit her.

She lives across seas and there are so many obstacles, discouraging voices.

He won't listen to them.

He will take her flowers; she likes flowers. He will arrange them for her though he is not skilled at arrangements.

When they turn her she will see the flowers, different ones on each side.

He will make her soup, she likes soup. He will cook mushroom and chicken soup, pour off the juice so it's easy to swallow.

He will sit close by so she can see him from her bed without moving.

He will ask her to smile and she will smile for him. She will ask him to turn on the radio so she can hear music, maybe Vivaldi or Mozart.

They will talk, but not very much. She will fix her eyes on him, the long look of longing.

He'll make an office upstairs and when she sleeps he will go there and work, forget for a while.

But he doesn't like to hear her cry out when she's turned.

He'll go upstairs each day when it's time for the turning, shut the door, lie down, close his eyes.

Aftermaths

Already the cold wind of something new and nameless is calling you.

You listen, you don't respond.

You want this moment to vaporise, you want it to extend endlessly.

That morning, the stairs, you couldn't run down them quickly enough. She had opened her eyes. 'They all do.'

You snip off some of her hair and put it in an envelope. Someone labels it.

He had told you to open the windows. You didn't want to hear this, but no doubt it was necessary.

You don't feel relief, some do. You don't feel numb, some do.

The night before she had smiled for the first time in several days and you thought, she has decided to give up. But she is saying to us, 'you have done what you can, it's OK.'

The night before the sitter didn't turn up, so you made a makeshift bed beside her.

In a drawer you find them golden and unfaded: the plaits she scissored off you, rescued from the floor.

Ubasuteyama

winds the story

when a Japanese woman was seventy years old
her son would take her up the mountain
on his back
and leave her there to die
ubasuteyama

throwing away grandma mountain
mountain throwing grandmother away
some say it was an ancient custom
some say it was only a folktale
bones discarded blind hill graveyard knowing

how did her afterglow find its way?
did it rise to the clouds?
did it slide down the slope?

imagine the cold at night
picture the pitch black
of abandoning your mother

one old woman when she was carried up
plucked twigs and scattered
a wavering trail
so her son could trace his path back

the luminous tale that Buddhists tell

grandma throwing mountain away
discarded graveyard growing

The Women of Calama

she undresses
but finds
her flesh has fled

their heaviness
thrown alive in the ocean

what can detain us?

no more disappeared, only dead people
no more disappeared, no prosecutions

the Chilean women of Calama
thrash through the sands
hunting their brothers
sons, husbands

the mothers of the Plaza de Mayo
white headscarves embroidered
cover their heads with
the names of the murdered

evacuation eradication

the Atacama desert

dinosaur fossils
a mass grave
a mummified Mayan

traces of bone
dissolved in solution

the women sift sands for their children
the childless take spades to their mothers' childhoods

she watched her mother
in the desert walking
conversing with her mother
and father recalling

voices held in stuttering detention
the residue of hallucinations

women with shovels
plastic bags full of bones
DNA testing

no more disappeared, only dead people
no more disappeared, no prosecutions

you're dead she said
until you wake up

the child you once were
dismembered as wailing

when his bones were returned
all she could do was
kiss his remains
re-assemble her mourning

crushed bones, a mass grave
flowers thrown in the air

Siteless

The calmness grips me tight but lets me breathe. I am on the edge of understanding, though I don't know what I need to understand.

This is the place you find when you reach the other side of panic. You are the *Man on Wire*, but if you topple, the ground will be waiting for you, soft.

All my life she said, I've worried about the future and regretted the past. The only absorption I've known is my own distraction. I've wallowed in unease. He always put the converse point of view. Maybe those who claim otherwise, he said, are lying.

I had listened over and over again but I hadn't really *heard* anything. There were body parts strewn all over a field. Then I cocked up my ear, the lovesick leant towards each other, and soon the dead were awkwardly, but harmoniously, walking.

There was a process here, the result was pure immersion, but I didn't know if it arose from accumulation or erasure. I was on the veranda looking out. Even then I was beginning to worry the mountains would disappear or that this was happening because my hearing seemed to be failing.

Knowing someone isn't the same as entering their space. You can't log on by imagining the password. You find the doors don't slide. You can phone in but you can't guarantee who'll be answering.

If I met you in another world, the eyeless woman said, I might not know your face but I'd recognise your calmness, now that's unique. Your calmness, if only I could wear it like a shirt or adopt it as a skin. Your calmness, so convincing, it's almost three-dimensional.

The eyeless woman is fumbling. She seems to be finding walls. But there are also gaps where the sides slant but don't absolutely meet. Why can't she go through?

She recognises this space, once in an earlier life she has seen it in a film. It is Tarkovsky, yes it's *Stalker*, but without the abjection! She must be in the Zone. If she can match up the spaces, and find the exit, she'll be safe. Maybe it isn't a film at all. Perhaps she's in *Vox 5*: a patching together of sounds snatched from different spheres: seagulls, sea, desert, fields. Mashed together with traces of breath, stammerings of the primordial.

It could be about birth or the birth of language. It melts bodies into dung. They throw their passports over their heads to dodge the barbed wire boundaries.

Her greatest fear had always been that when she died she would still be conscious, but unable to speak. Alive but written off, prone and silent on a table.

The Decision

A decision had to be made, and because he was very old she felt she had to make it for him. There was a diagnosis that was irrefutable. There were pressures for and against: if he did not have the operation it was certain death, but that death would probably be slow, he might live for many more months, even years. If he had the operation he might recover and live a great deal longer, but it was a risk because of his age. It was in the days when doctors didn't tell patients the truth because they thought it might frighten them. Or, at least, their close relatives had to make a decision whether they should be told or not.

Some thought you should never lie to anyone, others thought that you should try to ease suffering even if it meant lying. Some believed that being lied to was itself a form of suffering, because people always knew they were being lied to, and because not knowing – when it involved your whole future – was worse than knowing, however terrible that knowing might be. The doctors said they took the cue from the patient. Some patients asked and some didn't. If they inquired, you told them. If they didn't, you kept it to yourself. This was all a long time ago, before doctors were worried about whether they would be sued for misinformation, and before patients were considered to be fully in charge of their own lives.

Some thought it was best to have a quick death to avoid pain and suffering, but others thought it was important not to abort life and to make sure everyone lived for as long as possible. Many thought you couldn't make those kinds of decisions on behalf of another, and that any vicarious decision was wrong.

She had always thought a quick death would be the best kind of exit, but now, suddenly, that didn't seem so clearly the case. Once you died you were over the line, so maybe it was best to push back the line for as long as possible.

It was surprising how fuzzy matters of life and death could be. Death was final, inevitable and non-negotiable, but the exact moment at which it occurred could be delayed, almost decided. It was as if you could determine the moment of death for yourself or, more alarmingly, someone else could settle it for you without your knowledge. Every day such choices were forced on people by other people.

Some people thought that a decision of this type was not really a decision because you were being advised. If you were being advised, that took the responsibility off you.

When he had the operation, the first phone call said it had been successful. The second phone call said he had died. She could only think one thought: she had thrown the wrong dice. She had not pushed back the line. She had failed to help him.

It was a father who brought a daughter into the world but it was a daughter who decided when her father left it.

At first it seemed as if the guilt, the anguish, the wish to rewind would never find an alternative target. She would wake in the morning, and sometimes the thought would not be present for a few moments, but then it would return.

Some said that she was deliberately inviting it in and giving it too much leg-room. These were the people who believed in willpower. With willpower, they said, you could turn anything away. But she knew that willpower didn't work. Willpower was contrary. Whichever way you told it to move, it preferred the other way.

She asked herself questions that could not be answered, though she couldn't stop posing them. There was always that hope, if you answered the question, it would slip away. But questions didn't move aside just because you wanted them to. And even if someone said, *It is no good thinking about that, because it cannot be changed*, you couldn't stop thinking about something just because it was irreversible.

She went over and over the diagnosis. Maybe it was not as irrefutable as it had seemed. Any diagnosis was subjective and could not be trusted. There was no second opinion. The doctor seemed pleasant but inexperienced, should she have really put her faith in him?

Some people did not talk to her about it. They were either not interested or they were, but they waited for her to raise the topic. Sometimes she did raise it. They said that sometimes you had to take a decision and it had certain consequences. But you couldn't always know what those consequences would be. You couldn't be held responsible for what followed. Most people said that whatever she had concluded it wouldn't have mattered because he was dying anyway.

She felt alone because she had made the decision. You could read about other people who made similar choices and that did help, but their problem was never exactly the same. The news was full of mistakes that people had made. But maybe those decisions were just like this dilemma, and had to be made without knowing what needed to be known.

Everything was directed at making the feeling lessen. When she went away on holiday it was less, when she went shopping it was less, when she went for dinner with people it was less. She was told to talk about it, but talking about it didn't necessarily help.

Then one day, many years later, her daughter said to her, *But of course it was the right decision, he didn't suffer, he was asleep and didn't know anything. He was neurotic about his health and you saved him months of suffering. And anyway you were advised to do it, and if you hadn't followed that guidance, it would have been reckless.*

Maybe it had been said before, maybe it was said at the right moment when she was recovering anyway and was more receptive to it, maybe it was the way it was said, but she felt she had been acquitted. Maybe she hadn't been so wrong after all. Maybe she hadn't been to blame. From this moment her recovery ran its course, slow and halting, and with many minor reversals. Recovery was not resolution. Recovery was having a glimmer that in the end it didn't make that much difference. A few more weeks of life were not much on top of a long, long life that had run its course.

She didn't always believe this, but at certain moments she did.

She wondered if it would be passed through the generations. Not her guilt and fear, but the inevitability of this situation arising again. Her daughter would suffer it, and her granddaughter, and it would go on and on. It would always be there, the possibility of its regeneration. One day someone might make a decision on her behalf like this. Maybe the same one. Maybe a different type of decision she couldn't at the moment imagine. Or maybe she would, knowing all this, intercede: take the decision herself.

Notes

Experimentalism: 'Experimentalism' was inspired by the documentary *Forgiving Dr Mengele*, 2006, directed by Bob Hercules and Cheri Pugh, USA. It concerned Eva Mozes Kor, a Holocaust victim who decided to forgive the Nazis. Eva, and her twin sister Miriam, survived Josef Mengele's extremely dangerous medical experiments at Auschwitz. They were separated from their parents and older sisters in the concentration camp and never saw them again.

The Great Egret: This poem was written for the Bimblebox 153 Birds Project, a developing project around the 153 bird species that have been recorded on the Bimblebox Nature Refuge in the Desert Uplands Bioregion of Central West Queensland, Australia. The home of these birds, and the ecosystems that support them, is in the path of a proposed coal mine. The poem was also inspired by the wedding scene in the film, *The Suspended Step of the Stork*, 1991, directed by Theodoros (Theo) Angelopoulos, Greece. In the scene a couple marry across the banks of a river that flows through a divided country.

Blow-up: This poem was inspired by a seminar given by Jessica Whyte, 'Human Rights: Confronting Governments? Michel Foucault and the Right to Intervene' at Western Sydney University in 2012, and her 2012 article '"Intervene, I Said"', *Overland*, 207 www.overland.org.au/previous-issues/issue-207/feature-jessica-whyte.

Feasting on Belshazzar: This poem is dedicated to my niece, Emma Rivlin. It refers to a performance she directed of Handel's opera *Belshazzar*, and to elements of the story of the libretto. In the biblical tale on which the libretto is based, the visionary Daniel interpreted the writing on the wall, 'Mene, Mene, Tekel, Upharsin', as the imminent end for the Babylonian kingdom. Trinity Laban Opera performed the work at Blackheath Halls in London. The performance I attended was on July 5th 2014.

Feisty and Childless (an internet cut and paste): This piece uses conceptual poetry techniques. It morphs the 'cut up' into the 'cut and paste' by combining snippets from newspaper articles, interactive forums and academic discourses about voluntary childlessness, found through Google searching. Sources for the poem include *The Age, The Drum, Jezebel, The Daily Mail* and *The Childless By Choice Survey*, 2004–6, www.childlessbychoiceproject.com/Childless_by_Choice_Survey.html. Other sources were Daniel Gilbert, 2007, *Stumbling on Happiness*, New York: Vintage and Rosemary Gillespie, 2000, 'When No Means No: Disbelief, Disregard and Deviance as Discourses of Voluntary Childlessness', Women's Studies International Forum 23 (2): 223–234.

The Bleeding Obvious (an internet cut and paste): This prose poem, another internet cut and paste, combined snippets (sometimes modified) from the following sources: Cecil Adams, 2008, 'How Do Female Astronauts Menstruate in Space?', *The Straight Dope*, November 28, www.straightdope.com/columns/read/2827/how-do-female-astronauts-menstruate-in-space.

Janet Allon, 2013, 'Adventures in Menstruation: Time to Dump those Silly Taboos', *AlterNet*, March 31, www.alternet.org/adventures-menstruation-time-dump-those-silly-taboos.

Katie J.M. Baker, 2013, 'All Hail the World's First Menstrual Poetry Slam', *Jezebel*, May 22, www.jezebel.com/all-hail-the-worlds-first-menstrual-poetry-slam-509335746.

Hannah Betts, 2013, 'The P Word: a Last Taboo', *The Telegraph*, October 28, www.telegraph.co.uk/women/womens-life/10401952/Periods-A-last-taboo-Why-the-hell-cant-we-talk-about-them.html.

Hannah Betts, 2014, 'The P Word', *Daily Life*, July 6, www.dailylife.com.au/health-and-fitness/dl-wellbeing/the-p-word-20140703-3bb36.html.

Gary DeMar, 2014, 'Crazy Feminists Want Their "Period" to Bleed "Freely" and Feminize Wikipedia', *Godfather Politics*, February 5, www.godfatherpolitics.com/14262/crazy-feminists-want-period-bleed-freely-feminize-wikipedia/#hkwztFP45lWLOyo9.99.

Megan Hicks, Undated, 'The Rags: Paraphernalia of Menstruation', Powerhouse Museum, www.powerhouse-museum.com/rags.

Erin Gloria Ryan, 2014, 'Lily Allen Says She's a Menstrual Music Pioneer', *Jezebel*, November 4, www.jezebel.com/lily-allen-says-shes-a-menstrual-music-pioneer-1562270841.

TutorCircle, Undated, 'What is Menstruation in Maths?', math.tutorcircle.com/geometry/what-is-menstruation-in-maths.html.

Catherine Yronwode, Undated, 'Body Fluids in Hoodoo: Menstrual Blood, Semen, and Urine', www.luckymojo.com/bodyfluids.html.

Wikipedia, Undated, 'Culture and Menstruation', www.en.wikipedia.org/wiki/Culture_and_menstruation.

Metaphorics: 'Metaphorics' is in three parts. The first section was written by cutting and pasting, with some modification, comments about metaphor from the internet. The sources were:

'Against Metaphor', Undated, *State of Emergency*, www.gauchesinister.wordpress.com/2010/10/12/against-metaphor.

AMD Pronunciation Studio, Undated, 'The 56 Worst Analogies from High School Papers', www.angmohdan.com/ 56-worst-analogies-high-school-papers.

Glenn Croman, Undated, 'The Power of the Tiger?', www2.yk.psu.edu/~jmj3/sc4_crom.htm.

Donald Campbell and Henrik Enckell, 2005, 'Metaphor and the Violent', *The International Journal of Psychoanalysis*, 86 (3): 802–23.

Richard A. Fumerton, 1995, *Metaepistemology and Skepticism*, Lanham: Rowman and Littlefield.

'Metaphors', Undated, 2014, *The Economist*, www.economist.com/style-guide/metaphors.

'What Is a Metaphor?', Undated, *About Education*, www.grammar.about.com/od/qaaboutrhetoric/f/faqmetaphor07.htm.

Judy Rees, Undated, *The Mind Reader's Guide To Metaphor*, www.udemy.com/the-mind-readers-guide-to-metaphor.

Ekaterina Shutova and Tony Veale, 2014, Tutorial: 'Computational Modelling of Metaphor', Conference of the European Chapter of the Association for Computational Linguistics, University of Gothenburg, Gothenburg, www.eacl2014.org/tutorial-metaphor.

Al Vernacchio, 2012, 'Sex Needs a New Metaphor: Here's one', *TED*, www.ted.com/talks/al_vernacchio_sex_needs_a_new_metaphor_here_s_one.

Martyn Frank Warren, 2008, 'Music as Metaphor: a Powerful Tool in Management Development', National Farm Management Conference, Oxford, www.researchgate.net/publication/235954865_Music_as_metaphor_a_powerful_tool_in_management_development.

The Blue Bus: 'The Blue Bus' was written for a poetry reading I gave at The Blue Bus experimental poetry reading series in London.

The Other Room: This poem was written as a tribute to the adventurous reading series in Manchester, The Other Room, run by Scott Thurston, Tom Jenks and James Davies. It refers to Haruki Murakami's 2013 book, *1Q84*, London: Vintage Books, in which there are two moons.

Art For Whose Sake?: This piece refers to a number of newspaper articles on the work of Mishka Henner. The main source is 'A Conversation with Mishka Henner', *Prison Photography*, www.prisonphotography.org/2012/04/23/a-conversation-with-mishka-henner.

Subvoices: This poem was written for a publication edited by Scott Thurston for British poet Robert Sheppard's sixtieth birthday. It refers to the Subvoicive experimental poetry reading series in London, founded and curated by Gilbert Adair in the 1980s and subsequently curated by Laurence Upton.

What You're Doing, If You Know: This poem is based on several closely related quotations from interviews with American theatre director Robert Wilson. See, for example, Tim Teeman's interview in 2012, 'Robert Wilson: "Your island is so cut off. It's very provincial"', *The Times*,

August 1, www.timteeman.com/2012/08/01/robert-wilson-your-island-is-so-cut-off-its-very-provincial. Wilson says, 'One reason to be an artist is to say "What is it?", not what it is. If you know what you're doing, there's no reason doing it. Everything should remain open-ended.'

Tilt: The quotation 'Unsettling transfiguration of once-familiar terrain' is from page one of Joan Retallack's 2003 book, *The Poethical Wager*, Berkeley: University of California Press.

Ubasuteyama: Ubasuteyama is about the practice in medieval Japan of *ubasuteyama* (grandmother throwing mountain), whereby an elderly relative was taken up a mountain and left to die. The practice was most common in times of hardship caused by famine or drought, and was the basis of a fascinating film *The Ballad of Narayama* by Shōhei Imamura, Japan, 1983. The poem also alludes to a Buddhist allegory about an old woman who was taken up the mountain and scattered twigs to help her son find his way back.

The Women of Calama: This poem refers to 'the disappeared' in both Chile and Argentina, and the reactions of the wives and mothers of those killed. Influential on the poem was an article by Zoe Crossland, 2000, 'Buried Lives: Forensic Archaeology and the

Disappeared in Argentina', *Archaeological Dialogues* 7 (2): 146–159.

Siteless: Siteless refers to 'Vox 5', a voice-based composition by Trevor Wishart, 1990, *Vox*, Virgin Records, CD, VC 7 91108–2.

Acknowledgements

Some of these poems have been published, sometimes in a different version or as part of longer pieces, in *Australian Poetry Journal, Cordite Poetry Review, Ekleksographia, Electronic Overland, Gangway, Hyperrhiz, Mascara Literary Review, Otoliths, Poetry New Zealand, Scan, Seizure, Southerly, Stride, Text, The Other Room Anthologies 5 and 7*, and on the ABC *Soundproof* website.

My warm thanks to Ivor Indyk for his sensitive, in-depth engagement with my work, and for all his expert editorial advice, and to Alice Grundy for her excellent and cheerful editorial assistance. My thanks, also, to my friend and long-time collaborator Sieglinde Karl-Spence for giving permission to use a striking image of her artwork on the cover of the book. I am very grateful to my current and previous colleagues in the Writing and Society Research Centre at Western Sydney University for creating a stimulating work environment and the members of austraLYSIS, especially Roger Dean, Greg White, Sandy Evans, Phil Slater and Will Luers, for their inspiration and collaboration. I also thank all the many other friends, relatives, students and colleagues who have encouraged and helped me. In particular, I would like to express gratitude to Anne Brewster for her strong interest in, and advice about, my work over nearly two decades; Joy Wallace for her intensive involvement with my poetry and for writing so perceptively about it and ceramicist, Joanna Still, for her collaboration and conversation. Roger Dean has read more than one draft of the volume and has made numerous telling suggestions.